Conversations with the Saints

By

Dr. Lydia A. Woods

CWP

Channing and Watt Publishers
Atlanta, GA

Other Publications by Dr. Lydia A. Woods

Acceptance with Joy
Poems by Revelation
For the Edification of the Saints
Food for Saints
Let Those With Ears…
All the Saints Agree
Those Bible Characters
Lessons of a Handmaiden
The Movies: Their Spiritual Messages
The Joy of the Lord
Under the Rainbow

Dedicated to
My Beloved Brothers...
William and Gene

Acknowledgements

A piece of creative work is usually produced in isolation, but the distribution for others to see and appreciate takes many hearts and hands and minds. I want to give thanks to my friends and family members who are those hearts which support and lift me up and forward.

Special thanks to William C. Terry, Yehonatan Meru, and Veronica Norris for taking their time to proofread this book.

My appreciation to the host of colleagues, students and fellow Christian brothers and sisters who praise and encourage me and constantly remind me of the work God can do in a willing but frightened and fragile vessel.

Thank you Holy Spirit for using my humble vessel
and letting me put my name on these words.

Introduction

Under the inspiration of the Holy Spirit, I began writing Christian Poetry. When I look back at the beginning, I realize now that I knew very little about the Holy Spirit and His relationship to me. At first, I would be awakened during the night, out of a sound sleep, with a poem forming in my head, or sometimes while driving, or in the midst of conversation with someone.

I would tell people that the Spirit would come and go, then months later return, to give me poems. My understanding has since grown, and I now know that the Spirit never leaves and is always present with me and in me and thru me – the two of us are one.

I believe the Holy Spirit, is God and that God exists in every human being. The real gift of life is discovering God within you, which first blesses you, then those around you.

These collections of poems are inspired by the lessons which the Lord has been teaching me as I walk with Him. Many poems are inspired by uplifting and stimulating conversations with God's precious Saints and others are born out of the frustration that many do not know the Love of God and His amazing grace and mercy.
In reading, I hope you will find poems which speak to your heart, express what you have experienced, or have enlightened your understanding. The writing of these poems allow me an outlet of spiritual expression, as the Lord tempers and prepares me for my Calling.

Table of Contents

Poems

Scriptural References

Poems

Dr. Lydia A. Woods

Ain't He All That!

Hebrews 1:2-3; John 1:1-5; Revelation 22:13 (KJV)

You've heard the young people say…
That he or she "Ain't all that,"
I know One whose "All That" and that's a fact.

Ain't He All That – and then some.
He's Alpha and Omega the Holy One.

Ain't He All That – and that's for sure,
Sent for the Salvation of man – earth's cure.

Ain't He All That – and you know why?
Cause He's the only One that can satisfy.

Ain't He All That – just look around you and attest,
He's head and heels over all the rest.

Ain't He All That – He can take away pain,
Heal broken hearts, save sinners with no strain.

Ain't He All That – a place to safely run,
In times of trouble, He's the only One.

Ain't He All That – for the care and love,
He's all that – Our Father above!

- Conversation with Ms. Elizabeth J. Jackson

A Blessing – Not a Curse!

Psalm 127:3-5 (KJV)

It is written, children are a Blessing not a curse,
But a bunch of kids – What could be worse?

They suck your time and money, kill your dreams,
It's a long hard haul, and so it seems.

That for the present I wonder how and why,
These kids will bless me by and by.

To sacrifice your life's blood - And children just take,
At times it seems having them was a big mistake.

If you've walked that path you know what I mean,
Especially, if you have survived the teens!

Each stage brings joys, frustrations and fears,
Will they ever mature -- These little dears?

But if you ask me if I'd do it all again,
Without a doubt I would answer, yes, my friend.

-3-

Cause when I beheld my new precious grandson,
I knew deep joy and gladness had really begun.

I never realized that the next step would be,
Generations through my seed for me to see,

A strange feeling of happiness in God's plan,
To bring generations through the seed of man,

Being a door to life, is worth all the pain,
The plan is quite amazing and simple to explain.

That a bunch of kids - What could be worse?
Children are a blessing -- Not a curse!

- Conversation with Mr. Gene Wideman

Call My Name

I Peter 2:9 (KJV)

The Lord allows you to put some living under your belt,
Before He calls your name and His urging is felt.

He first set His love on you – not the other way round,
So don't think it's your idea – when the Lord you have found.

He calls you out of darkness into His marvelous light,
In the Lamb's Book of Life your name He writes.

But you can't accept Him as your Lord, until that day,
You must wait on the Lord, before you can say.

"Lord come into my life, change me, save me, please,"
So until that time, you are just one of these.

One of the lost sheep, waiting to be found,
But the shepherd hasn't forgotten, soon you'll be kingdom bound.

He'll leave the ninety-nine on your behalf,
And you'll soon be guided by His rod and staff,

The Angels will rejoice and many Saints too,
The moment you take Him for your own and say – I do.

Until your name is called many Saints water and plant,
But God gives the increase, so I repeat – You can't!

Just take the Lord any time as your Savior to proclaim,
You must wait your turn, until – He Calls Your Name!

                              - Conversation with Ms. Delores Johnson

Cerebral Palsy

Philippians 1:6; I Thessalonians 5:24; I Corinthians 1:9 (KJV)

For a parable of the present day Church, I'll need,
To borrow Cerebral Palsy, as an example, please.

The brain sends signals for the body to heed,
But the limbs don't follow the brain's careful lead.

One leg goes sideways when it should go straight,
One arm goes left or right when it should wait,

The head it jerks, the trunk is not quite right,
Every body part is trying with all its might.

To follow the directions coming from the head,
But something is wrong there is confusion instead.

Where there is confusion, every work of Satan can be found,
The Body of Christ looks to the world like a foolish clown.

Seems to me this interference must be moved out of the way,
For the Church to function perfectly as it should, today.

Jesus is our hope and He's coming you can bet,
And that interference will be put in a lake that is not wet!

- Conversation with Ms. Gloria Roe

Common Sense

I Corinthians 1:25, 3:19; II Corinthians 5:7; Proverbs 3:5-6 (KJV)

"You know God gave us, "common sense,"
People say this every day,
But it's not common sense we need,
But faith in God, to help us find our way,

Make no mistake about the world,
With its rules and hatred for God's Word,
Trying to figure it out with your head,
Is a fruitless venture – I have heard.

For the Word says the foolishness of God,
Will confound the wisdom of man,
His ways and thoughts are not ours,
We need faith and the Holy Spirit to understand.

For without faith as your sixth sense,
You will perish in your sin,
Using "common sense" and reason,
In this earth realm you can never win.

Lean not to thy own understanding,
That is "common sense" to me,
Don't rely on the "common sense," of this world,
That will never lead to life or eternity.

- Conversation with Ms. Gloria Roe

Convicted

Romans 7:14-25 (KJV)

Satan is good at what he does - make no mistake,
Setting up Saints to partake, of his evil bait.

After the first bite of his delicious cake,
You curse your very life - your flesh you hate.

I'd been walking with the Lord so very long,
I didn't believe I could do, this kind of wrong,

I know the Word, so very well,
How could I do this thing, from the pit of hell?

You immediately feel sick, you know what I mean,
The pleasure you thought you'd have from doing the thing,

Only leaves' you broken, feeling you have betrayed,
Your heavenly Father – it's the saddest of days.

You want to turn the clock back, just a little bit,
Repeat the decision, 'cause you have been tricked.

Fallen for the trap, of the evil one,
Lord forgive the weakness, in your daughters and sons.

But the Lord has made provision, 'cause he knows us well,
In His Son, who has the keys to the Kingdom and hell.

-9-

It is written,
"Repent and turn away from your sin,"
He'll forgive you and salvation is yours, in the end.

Yes, He will forgive you, but you have a price to pay,
Forgiving yourself often gets in your way.

It's hard to move past, that sin you've committed,
But one day in your testimony, you'll gladly admit it.

That you fell that time, but the Lord was good,
It made you a better person, and you understood,

That what was meant for evil, God turned to your good,
And His purpose was accomplished, as it should.

But the conviction of the Holy Spirit – we all will feel,
'Cause the Father loves His children, and that's for real!

He chastises those He calls His own, and that is why,
You should take comfort at this time, that you Qualify!

- Conversation with Mr. Vestell C. Royal

Denominations

Mark 3:24-25; I Corinthians 12:12-31 (KJV)

Denominations whose brilliant plan is this?
It's surely not God's – I must insist.

It has the markings of you-know-who,
Cause it divides Christians – me against you.

Now how crazy it all seems to me,
Serving the same God, but we can't agree!

You interpret the Word this way not that,
We differ on almost every single fact.

Our denomination has all the truth, over here,
And our group is going in – not yours, my dear.

A house divided on itself shall surely fall,
Jesus taught this in His Word to one and all.

I look forward to the day when denominations cease,
And the Body of Christ works for God's purpose in peace.

Serving one God must include one single plan,
And in this plan denominations cannot ultimately stand.

The enemy is good at trying to destroy,
By dividing us with this denominational ploy.

Lord, we wait patiently, searching the heavens above,
Looking for that perfect ending of unity in love.

- Conversation with Mr. William C. Terry

-11-

Forgive or Forgive Not

Luke 6:37; Mark 11:25-26 (KJV)

Forgive or forgive not, the choice is up to you.
But choose wisely and carefully, whatever you do!

For to forgive not - can seal your very fate,
By eating you alive, with a cancer of consuming hate.

But to forgive - now you're talking my language here,
The sweetest of gestures, frees your Spirit, my dears!

He's Good At...

Genesis 1:3, 9, 12, 16, 24, 27, 31; Isaiah 14:27, 46:9-11 (KJV)

He's good – you've got to give it to Him,
Didn't need help creating angels, man or cherubim,

He's good – 'cause He made all that you see,
Canyons, flowers, bugs, rivers and the mighty tree.

He's good at – making the sun,
The moon, skies and stars every one,

He's good at – making mountains and lakes,
He's just good for goodness sake,

He's good at – making women and men,
And loving them in spite of their constant sin,

He's good at – accomplishing His own plan,
Through the lives of any woman, child, or man.

He's good at – what He does,
That's why we are here and He's above.

He's good at – solving our little messes,
That He turns into our greatest successes.

He's good at – blessing us too,
I'm trying to figure how -- He do what He do!

He's good at – and He is -- All that!
So just accept that -- He's Good At!

                    - Conversation with Ms. Delores Johnson

-13-

If Thou Be...

Matthew 4:6 (KJV)

If thou be the Son of God,
Satan's question to Jesus -- Now that was odd!

Satan knew He was the only begotten Son,
Was he just fooling around, having a bit of fun?

Is Satan so stupid or something worse,
To expect Jesus to serve him and His Father curse?

Jesus came to do the Father's Will,
And Satan knew it -- so what's the deal?

Now I've always thought Satan, not to bright,
To question Jesus on the issue of His birthright,

And if he would question Jesus with so stupid a plan,
Then he'll put the question to any ordinary woman or man.

Yes, Satan questions our birthright day in and out,
Trying to cause confusion and set up doubt.

And his stupid plan has worked like a charm,
Saints are giving him power and being disarmed.

Questioning their birthright has caused many to doubt,
They have power to foil his plan and wipe him out.

Power given to them through the Holy Name,
Step up with faith and your birthright claim.

So that whosoever that believes in Him,
Can through faith in Jesus their Salvation win.

And when Satan questions -- If Thou Be ...
Say, It is Written -- and there is no doubt in me!

                                        - Conversation with Ms. Serena Reese

If You Will Be Great

Matthew 20:26; I Peter 5:3 (KJV)

If you will be great, a servant you'll be,
That's what Jesus told the disciples – trust me.

The feet of them Jesus washed to make it clear,
That to be great in the kingdom – be a servant, my dear.

Now down here on earth, who plays the servant's part,
The job of a mother qualifies – she has a servant's heart.

She is the door of life into the earth, for the seed,
And she catches it most from the enemy, indeed.

She ministers to the least of these – you know,
The children in her care, she nurtures to grow.

In the end times many mothers have emerged strong,
Have taken the challenge to become Spiritually full grown.

Satan has attacked the family, and it's down on its knees,
But Jesus has the victory and He has the keys.

And a mere servant girl can beat the enemy to shame,
'Cause she has access to the keys and Jesus' precious name.

So mothers step up and receive your servant's pay,
You have a place of Honor in the Kingdom, Today!

- Conversation with Ms. Elizabeth J. Jackson

Just a Family Feud

Genesis 12:2, 17:6, 18:18 (KJV)

I was discussing with a Saint, about our Family Tree,
How big and flourishing, it must now surely be.

The family of humankind was our immediate concern,
The Holy Spirit came on board to help us learn.

We started from the beginning, just talking and mapping it so,
I wanted a huge wall to draw on to see how big it would grow.

There was Adam and Eve, Noah and his three sons,
Ham, Japheth and Shem, three great nations had begun.

Through Shem's line came our father Abraham with great faith,
With Ishmael and Isaac, two important nations in their place.

And of course through Isaac the Promise manifested,
Our Lord and Savior Jesus Christ was begot and then tested.

He was found pure, a proper unblemished Lamb, God's man,
Then sacrificed to redeem us all as part of the glorious plan.

The gentiles given a chance to become children by faith,
Those born of Abraham's seed, also redeemed by grace.

It's "Just a Family Feud," and who do you think is winning?
Well, I can tell you this, one day it will all stop – This sinning!

We must remember, family members, are noted for their love,
One to another, which pleases their heavenly Father above.

We are all of one family serving the One True God,
No matter what you call Him – now isn't that odd.

That we should all be fighting for an inheritance and a place,
In God's Holy presence - One day we'll all stand face to face.

Brothers and sisters of every kindred and race,
Each in His kingdom by our Father's Mercy and Grace.

- Conversation with Mr. William C. Terry

Dr. Lydia A. Woods

The Kingdom is Like Unto...

Matthew 4:23, 13:10-11, 13:31-33, 20:1-16, 24:14, 25:1-30 (KJV)

"The Kingdom is Like Unto," is what Jesus proclaimed,
And they that heard His words would never be the same.

He testified of a place He knew that was glorious and fine.
So different from anything people had heard at that time.

Over and over examples of the Kingdom and its glory,
Why so many references, story after story?

It must have been very important for us to know,
For to the multitudes He taught them just so.

He taught them in parables, and the disciples inquired,
The meanings in private and He granted their desire.

He explained to the disciples that those with ears,
Would understand and take hope from their fears.

He told the disciples that they should take heed,
And understand the parable of the "Sower and the Seed,"

-21-

A Collection of Christian Poems   *The Kingdom is Like Unto...*

For in this one, all parables they could understand,
That they were blessed above many a righteous man.

The prophets and righteous men desired to see those things,
That Jesus taught and the freedom – Kingdom brings.

So why aren't we following Jesus' lead today?
Teaching in parables and on the Kingdom way,

The Kingdom is like unto... – It was good enough back then,
Making citizens of the Kingdom of women and men.

Jesus has come into His Kingdom it's here on earth,
Through every man, woman and child in the new birth.

If we practice Kingdom living in this earth, we'll live to tell,
How we overthrew Satan and stormed the gates of hell.

- Inspired By
Hannah Hunnard - Thank you for your precious books!

Love You - Not Your Sin

Romans 1:26-27 (KJV)

Just recently in the news the other day,
A discussion of what the Church had to say.

Gay and lesbian lifestyles all the rage,
But God's Word warns us on almost every page,

In the latter days humans will disregard what I say,
Heap to themselves teachers in the modern day.

Those who interpret to please their own mind,
Justifying their sin, leaving righteousness behind.

Now come on Church let's get back to the basics,
Let not sin rule us today in the Holy places.

That Holy place, where God resides is the temple,
It's not too difficult, but really quite simple.

The temple where I reside is within you,
So put away the sin you were born to.

Set aside your sin, do not fulfill the lust,
For to reign with Me you - Just must!

Each of us are born into sin,
Some sin more obvious to condemn,

Each of us struggling to live holy and pure,
And to bear our cross, overcome and endure.

Never the person should the Church condemn,
For God loves us -- but not our sin.

- Conversation with Mr. Gene Wideman

Only Human!

II Corinthians 5:17, 6:16 (KJV)

People will say, "You know you're only human."
Justifying the mistakes they make,
But if you are born again as I am,
I'm a "new creature" for heaven's sake.

I get a little irritated,
It gets under my skin for sure,
I no longer see myself as human,
But a creature full of power, holy and pure.

With what is dwelling on the inside of me,
I no longer qualify for the human race,
I've been elevated above the earth,
No longer functioning in time and space.

For the Spirit realm is my home,
I wage war on the enemies of God,
He has prepared me for such a fight,
We are a peculiar people, strange and odd.

This "New Creature" has wondrous power,
Over Satan and all spiritual beings from hell,
I just want to scream, we're no longer human,
I want to run and to everyone tell.

-25-

This new creature has been commanded to go,
Into all of the world and proclaim,
That the kingdom is come here on earth,
Through Jesus Christ we will never be the same.

Jesus has all power and the keys,
To heaven and earth and hell's gates,
So accept the Spirit let it come in,
A new creature is what it's gonna take,

To live in this world no ordinary humans,
To stand, and then stand, in that evil day,
Take hold of God's awesome mighty plan,
Which provides for His victory in this way.

He will dwell in these Holy temples,
In the last days, not made with hands,
Creating New Creatures in Jesus Christ,
Out of plain ordinary Humans!

Pro-Choice?

Mark 3:4; Exodus 20:13 (KJV)

You had "Pro-Choice" without a doubt,
But now you don't want to stick it out.

You laid right down and did that thing,
Knowing full well what that action might bring.

Your "Pro-choice" created a precious human life,
But now it's causing too much worldly strife.

Now your "Pro-choice" is this life to take,
'Cause you want the "Pro-choice" to separate.

It's my body and I don't want to share,
But of this sin you must beware.

Now to both – that body of yours is needed,
Both with rights to life unimpeded.

The law of man must protect each side,
So I'm afraid for nine months you must abide.

"Pro-Choice" you had it at first to make,
Your second "Pro-choice" we can't allow you to take!

- Conversation with Mr. Gene Wideman

-27-

Puzzling

Genesis 1:26 (KJV)

I've always enjoyed a good puzzle, you know,
The whole family round the table, enjoying it so.

Especially, round the holidays when it's very cold,
Off to the store for a puzzle, so my story goes.

Now the five hundred pieces we finish in a night,
The one thousand pieces, now that's a challenging sight.

A couple of day's work but we knock it out just fine,
Fitting pieces together – Stimulating our minds.

Each working in their little corner or space,
Grabbing at pieces sometimes it seems like a race.

I like looking for that little splash of yellow or red,
On the corner of her hat or the cover on the bed.

I like seeing it all somehow take form and shape,
Matching the picture on the box – Oh! I love to create!

A few more puzzles we finished this past holiday,
But it got me to thinking about the Lord's way.

I notice that life is like a giant puzzle you see,
God revealing the pieces of our lives – Now here's the key!

Suddenly, a piece is revealed clear to view,
It's fitted, then you see what was forming in you.

Now that only completes just a corner or section of you,
But I'm, always surprised 'cause I hadn't a clue.

Now a little more of the plan for your life is revealed,
One day the puzzle will be finished which once was concealed.

So now I understand that – I am the puzzle – There is a plan,
Scattered pieces being formed by the master's own hand.

He's working to complete my puzzle – Hurry please!
I'm trying to be patient, but I just want to see.

What will the likeness of my puzzle finally be,
Look child, it's the image of God – That I see!

- Conversation with Mr. Jeffrey Proctor and
Ms. Maria Kwiatkowski

Sabbath Day

Exodus 20:8-11; Luke 6:5 (KJV)

I recently had Saints ask me in seriousness,
Which day is Sabbath? Could you please address?

Is Sabbath Saturday or Sunday, can you tell me please?
I want to be in God's will – I want to appease!

I want to keep God's commandments in every way,
So could you please tell just which one is the day?

My response is one somewhat hard to understand,
For "Sabbath" is not a day – An explanation you demand?

For you have always been taught it was a "day,"
Let me explain it to you, just this way.

There are rituals and symbols in the Bible that conceal,
Hidden truths that are now to His Saints being revealed.

The hidden truths of "Sabbath" was revealed to me,
Now through the Holy Spirit, I want you to see.

-31-

"Sabbath" represents His precious Son, now can't you guess?
Created for man to relieve his labors on earth for perfect rest.

"Sabbath" was made for man, not the other way round.
Jesus is "Lord of the Sabbath," this is quite profound.

Jesus said, "come unto me ye who labor indeed,"
Your burden is heavy and in this world you will need,

One such as Me, who can give you relief,
From the labors of this world, I want you to cease.

He doesn't just want you to rest, in Him on only one day,
But every day in Jesus is God's perfect created way.

God sanctified and hallowed this precious day,
And only Jesus can be Holy and Sanctified in this way.

A "day" cannot be Holy, only the Christ – you'll realize,
So take this revelation knowledge and in this grow wise.

Be released from bondage to serving and esteeming a day,
And through Jesus our "Sabbath" know a more excellent way.

- Conversation with Mr. William C. Terry

Seeds of Self-Destruction

James 1:26, 3:5-10; Proverbs 18:21, 25:23 (KJV)

Seeds of self-destruction, planted when we're young,
The tender, innocent child, unaware that it's begun.

If the seeds of self-destruction take root and have their way,
Satan's plan will be accomplished in us today!

Parents, relatives, and friends are the willing ones,
They do Satan's bidding with their wagging foolish tongues.

Instead of building you up, they speak about your lack,
Your precious sensitive feelings get trampled, just like that!

The cruelty of those words, the acts of unkind deeds,
They all contribute to the growing of self-destruction seeds.

By the time you become adult, the seed has blossomed into a tree,
And there is ugly hideous fruit, growing in you and me.

The seeds are various kinds - I'll name them for you,
There is self-doubt, self-hatred, self-frustration now you have a clue.

They produce low self-esteem, lack of confidence, and the like,
Changing our appearance to fit some standard to be right.

-33-

A standard that is self-destructive it denies just who you are,
You look into the mirror - you've turned into something quite bizarre!

If the seeds of self-destruction, go according to the plan,
Then Satan only has to wait for the destruction of man,

But God has a plan too, that calls you into His marvelous light,
A slow process begins that will put you back to right.

For what Satan meant for evil to destroy, steal and kill,
We have a powerful weapon of defense – the human will.

And when we will to serve the Lord, we become new on the inside,
Those seeds of self-destruction can no longer in us abide.

The wicked plan has been overthrown; he is losing as I speak,
It sounded like a good one, but it was faulty and quite weak.

For no plan of self-destruction that Satan could ever think of,
Can stand against the forces of God's profound and precious love!

- Conversation with William C. Terry

Take No Thought

Luke 12:22-30 (KJV)

Take no thought – For what you should wear,
Take no thought – In this world of cares.

Take no thought – For your Father will provide.
If you'll only let Him – He will satisfy.

Take no thought – For where you should live.
Only learn that in any state you find yourself—Give!

Take no thought – For what you should eat,
For the Lord will supply your food, drink and meat.

Take no thought – For any need,
For He is faithful to fulfill this promise indeed.

Take no thought – I know it's easy to say,
But if you will practice, it's the only way,

Take no thought – Means to renew that mind,
Every day to achieve perfection divine.

Take no thought – Is the ultimate tribute indeed,
For without *Faith* it's impossible to please.

Take no thought – Is the only way to live down here,
Free from worry, disappointment, frustration and fear.

Take no thought, I'll say no more,
Just leave it all to the One we Adore!

There But For the Grace...

Luke 10:27-37; Matthew 22:39 (KJV)

There but for the Grace of God - Go I,
These words I've often wondered why?

How can the murderer, prostitute, drunk be me!
Look deeper friend and you will see.

There but for the Grace - Go you or I,
And so you ask the question ... Why?

That same question asked to the Master long ago,
Who is my neighbor? - Explain it so...

That I may know just who they are,
Are they near or are they far.

Love your neighbor as yourself, the great command,
My neighbor **is** myself, now I understand.

The inner being created just like me,
No differences that I can see!

I could be them - But for the Grace,
I see myself within every face.

I look into the souls of men,
I see myself reflected within,

So you are me and I am you,
From one God, one source, one family grew.

Compassion swells, I now know why,
There but for the Grace of God - Go I.

- Conversation with Mr. Gene Wideman

-36-

Tower of Babel

Genesis 11:1-10 (KJV)

The whole earth was of one same tongue,
And all could understand each and every one.

The people planned to make themselves a name,
To build a city and tower, to their own acclaim.

The Lord came down to see what they had done,
The city and tower they had begun.

He knew that being together and of one mind,
There was nothing to restrain – This humankind.

He confounded their speech – confusion set in,
Their evil plans went into a downward tailspin.

There is a lesson to be learned – So Church take heed,
One accord, one language is important for us to succeed.

Where there is division and confusion every work exists,
Of the enemy and his purpose to accomplish.

Denominations are just another "Tower of Babel," from old,
It scatters and divides us from accomplishing our goal.

Let's take heed from the Word that leads and guides,
To all wisdom and truth and in one mind abide.

- Conversation with Ms. Elizabeth J. Jackson

-37-

True Way of Life

John 13:34-35, 14:6 (KJV)

One day the Lord said to me,
When you think of Jesus what do you see?

I said, there is an image of a man in my mind,
Strong, gentle in spirit, loving and kind.

Then God said something that astonished me,
I'll forever change what you see.

He is not a man but something much more,
My Word will reveal what you missed before.

I am the Truth, the way and the life, He said.
Ponder this a moment inside your head.

Now say it all together, God said to me
I am a true way of life – Now what do you see?

Not a man, but a plan – A concept big and vast,
This answers some of my questions at last.

I was blown away –
My understanding was opened that day.
I wanted to hear more of what the Lord had to say.

He opened my understanding the light was bright in my head,
It was hard to take in all that He said.

If Jesus is a true way of life, then this means,
There is only One Way to enter that door it seems.

That "True Way of Life" is simple to understand,
Love God with your whole self and your fellow man.

Then you have lived that true life indeed,
And there is evidence that you are His seed.

Then one can enter through the door if the life is pure,
Because you truly know Jesus and that's for sure.

It's not about what a mouth will say,
It's about the evidence in your life from day to day.

I am the Truth, the Way and the Life – Live it and see,
Your life will tell if you really knew Me!

         - Conversation with Bill, Keith, and Rick

What's Your Problem?

Mark 16:15-18 (KJV)

If you have ever heard this man do his thing,
I'm talking about a precious Saint named, David Ring!

He gives a testimony that will surely inspire,
I listen to his tapes and never tire.

He was born the youngest in a family of seven,
A preacher's kid - a blessing from heaven.

He was born with cerebral palsy and his body was affected,
He suffered many things, was taunted and rejected.

His father went to be with the Lord – Oh how he cried,
And his sorrow was complete when his beloved mother died.

He wanted to die; his heart was broken and torn,
He lamented the day that he was born.

His sister was the only one, who didn't give up on him,
Like a good sister she nagged through thick and thin.

-41-

To get her off his back he went to church that day,
And Jesus changed his life in a mighty way.

The Lord healed his heart and called him to preach,
With his shaking body and jumbled speech.

Now he's preaching the Word of the gospel of Christ,
He's married with kids and a beautiful wife.

He reminds us all; who are healthy and strong,
That if he can work for the Kingdom - Then what is wrong?

My favorite part of his testimony is this,
As he convicts us all who would resist,

The call that the Lord has on each life, Your excuse can't stand,
"What's your problem healthy woman, healthy man!"

- Inspired by Mr. David Ring

Scriptural References

Dr. Lydia A. Woods

Ain't He All That!

Hebrews 1:2-3; John 1:1-5; Revelation 22:13 (KJV)

Hebrews 1:2-3 (KJV)
2 Hath in these last days spoken unto us by his Son, whom he hath appointed heir of all things, by whom also he made the worlds;
3 Who being the brightness of his glory, and the express image of his person, and upholding all things by the word of his power, when he had by himself purged our sins, sat down on the right hand of the Majesty on high:

John 1:1-5 (KJV)
1 In the beginning was the Word, and the Word was with God, and the Word was God.
2 The same was in the beginning with God.
3 All things were made by him; and without him was not any thing made that was made.
4 In him was life; and the life was the light of men.
5 And the light shineth in darkness; and the darkness comprehended it not.

Revelation 22:13 (KJV)
13 I am Alpha and Omega, the beginning and the end, the first and the last.

-45-

A Collection of Christian Poems   *Ain't He All That!*

A Blessing – Not a Curse!

Psalm 127:3-5 (KJV)

Psalm 127:3-5 (KJV)

[3] Lo, children are an heritage of the LORD: and the fruit of the womb is his reward.

[4] As arrows are in the hand of a mighty man; so are children of the youth.

[5] Happy is the man that hath his quiver full of them: they shall not be ashamed, but they shall speak with the enemies in the gate.

Dr. Lydia A. Woods

Call My Name

I Peter 2:9 (KJV)

I Peter 2:9 (KJV)
[9] But ye are a chosen generation, a royal priesthood, an holy nation, a peculiar people; that ye should shew forth the praises of him who hath called you out of darkness into his marvellous light;

-47-

Cerebral Palsy

Philippians 1:6; I Thessalonians 5:24; I Corinthians 1:9 (KJV)

Philippians 1:6 (KJV)
[6] Being confident of this very thing, that he which hath begun a good work in you will perform it until the day of Jesus Christ:

I Thessalonians 5:24 (KJV)
[24] Faithful is he that calleth you, who also will do it.

I Corinthians 1:9 (KJV)
[9] God is faithful, by whom ye were called unto the fellowship of his Son Jesus Christ our Lord.

Dr. Lydia A. Woods

Common Sense

I Corinthians 1:25, 3:19; II Corinthians 5:7; Proverbs 3:5-6 (KJV)

I Corinthians 1:25 (KJV)
25 Because the foolishness of God is wiser than men; and the weakness of God is stronger than men.

I Corinthians 3:19 (KJV)
19 For the wisdom of this world is foolishness with God. For it is written, He taketh the wise in their own craftiness.

II Corinthians 5:7 (KJV)
7 (For we walk by faith, not by sight:)

Proverbs 3:5-6 (KJV)
5 Trust in the LORD with all thine heart; and lean not unto thine own understanding.
6 In all thy ways acknowledge him, and he shall direct thy paths.

Convicted

Romans 7:14-25 (KJV)

Romans 7:14-25 (KJV)

[14] For we know that the law is spiritual: but I am carnal, sold under sin.

[15] For that which I do I allow not: for what I would, that do I not; but what I hate, that do I.

[16] If then I do that which I would not, I consent unto the law that it is good.

[17] Now then it is no more I that do it, but sin that dwelleth in me.

[18] For I know that in me (that is, in my flesh,) dwelleth no good thing: for to will is present with me; but how to perform that which is good I find not.

[19] For the good that I would I do not: but the evil which I would not, that I do.

[20] Now if I do that I would not, it is no more I that do it, but sin that dwelleth in me.

[21] I find then a law, that, when I would do good, evil is present with me.

[22] For I delight in the law of God after the inward man:

[23] But I see another law in my members, warring against the law of my mind, and bringing me into captivity to the law of sin which is in my members.

[24] O wretched man that I am! who shall deliver me from the body of this death?

[25] I thank God through Jesus Christ our Lord. So then with the mind I myself serve the law of God; but with the flesh the law of sin.

Denominations

Mark 3:24-25; I Corinthians 12:12-31 (KJV)

Mark 3:24-25 (KJV)

24 And if a kingdom be divided against itself, that kingdom cannot stand.
25 And if a house be divided against itself, that house cannot stand.

I Corinthians 12:12-31 (KJV)

12 For as the body is one, and hath many members, and all the members of that one body, being many, are one body: so also is Christ.
13 For by one Spirit are we all baptized into one body, whether we be Jews or Gentiles, whether we be bond or free; and have been all made to drink into one Spirit.
14 For the body is not one member, but many.
15 If the foot shall say, Because I am not the hand, I am not of the body; is it therefore not of the body?
16 And if the ear shall say, Because I am not the eye, I am not of the body; is it therefore not of the body?
17 If the whole body were an eye, where were the hearing? If the whole were hearing, where were the smelling?
18 But now hath God set the members every one of them in the body, as it hath pleased him.
19 And if they were all one member, where were the body?
20 But now are they many members, yet but one body.
21 And the eye cannot say unto the hand, I have no need of thee: nor again the head to the feet, I have no need of you.
22 Nay, much more those members of the body, which seem to be more feeble, are necessary:

-51-

23 And those members of the body, which we think to be less honourable, upon these we bestow more abundant honour; and our uncomely parts have more abundant comeliness.

24 For our comely parts have no need: but God hath tempered the body together, having given more abundant honour to that part which lacked.

25 That there should be no schism in the body; but that the members should have the same care one for another.

26 And whether one member suffer, all the members suffer with it; or one member be honoured, all the members rejoice with it.

27 Now ye are the body of Christ, and members in particular.

28 And God hath set some in the church, first apostles, secondarily prophets, thirdly teachers, after that miracles, then gifts of healings, helps, governments, diversities of tongues.

29 Are all apostles? are all prophets? are all teachers? are all workers of miracles?

30 Have all the gifts of healing? do all speak with tongues? do all interpret?

31 But covet earnestly the best gifts: and yet shew I unto you a more excellent way.

Forgive or Forgive Not

Luke 6:37; Mark 11:25-26 (KJV)

Luke 6:37 (KJV)
[37] Judge not, and ye shall not be judged: condemn not, and ye shall not be condemned: forgive, and ye shall be forgiven:

Mark 11:25-26 (KJV)
[25] And when ye stand praying, forgive, if ye have ought against any: that your Father also which is in heaven may forgive you your trespasses.
[26] But if ye do not forgive, neither will your Father which is in heaven forgive your trespasses.

-53-

He's Good At...

Genesis 1:3, 9, 12, 16, 24, 27, 31; Isaiah 14:27, 46:9-11 (KJV)

Genesis 1:3 (KJV)
3 And God said, Let there be light: and there was light.

Genesis 1:9 (KJV)
9 And God said, Let the waters under the heaven be gathered together unto one place, and let the dry land appear: and it was so.

Genesis 1:12 (KJV)
12 And the earth brought forth grass, and herb yielding seed after his kind, and the tree yielding fruit, whose seed was in itself, after his kind: and God saw that it was good.

Genesis 1:16 (KJV)
16 And God made two great lights; the greater light to rule the day, and the lesser light to rule the night: he made the stars also.

Genesis 1:24 (KJV)
24 And God said, Let the earth bring forth the living creature after his kind, cattle, and creeping thing, and beast of the earth after his kind: and it was so.

Genesis 1:27 (KJV)
27 So God created man in his own image, in the image of God created he him; male and female created he them.

Genesis 1:31 (KJV)
31 And God saw every thing that he had made, and, behold, it was very good. And the evening and the morning were the sixth day.

Isaiah 14:27 (KJV)
27 For the LORD of hosts hath purposed, and who shall disannul it? and his hand is stretched out, and who shall turn it back?

Isaiah 46:9-11 (KJV)

[9] Remember the former things of old: for I am God, and there is none else; I am God, and there is none like me,

[10] Declaring the end from the beginning, and from ancient times the things that are not yet done, saying, My counsel shall stand, and I will do all my pleasure:

[11] Calling a ravenous bird from the east, the man that executeth my counsel from a far country: yea, I have spoken it, I will also bring it to pass; I have purposed it, I will also do it.

If Thou Be...

Matthew 4:6 (KJV)

Matthew 4:6 (KJV)

[6] And saith unto him, If thou be the Son of God, cast thyself down: for it is written, He shall give his angels charge concerning thee: and in their hands they shall bear thee up, lest at any time thou dash thy foot against a stone.

If You Will Be Great

Matthew 20:26; I Peter 5:3 (KJV)

Matthew 20:26 (KJV)
26 But it shall not be so among you: but whosoever will be great among you, let him be your minister;

I Peter 5:3 (KJV)
3 Neither as being lords over God's heritage, but being examples to the flock.

Just a Family Feud

Genesis 12:2, 17:6, 18:18 (KJV)

Genesis 12:2 (KJV)
2 And I will make of thee a great nation, and I will bless thee, and make thy name great; and thou shalt be a blessing:

Genesis 17:6 (KJV)
6 And I will make thee exceeding fruitful, and I will make nations of thee, and kings shall come out of thee.

Genesis 18:18 (KJV)
18 Seeing that Abraham shall surely become a great and mighty nation, and all the nations of the earth shall be blessed in him?

The Kingdom is Like Unto...

Matthew 4:23, 13:10-11, 13:31-33, 20:1-16, 24:14, 25:1-30 (KJV)

Matthew 4:23 (KJV)

23 And Jesus went about all Galilee, teaching in their synagogues, and preaching the gospel of the kingdom, and healing all manner of sickness and all manner of disease among the people.

Matthew 13:10-11 (KJV)

10 And the disciples came, and said unto him, Why speakest thou unto them in parables?

11 He answered and said unto them, Because it is given unto you to know the mysteries of the kingdom of heaven, but to them it is not given.

Matthew 13:31-33 (KJV)

31 Another parable put he forth unto them, saying, The kingdom of heaven is like to a grain of mustard seed, which a man took, and sowed in his field:

32 Which indeed is the least of all seeds: but when it is grown, it is the greatest among herbs, and becometh a tree, so that the birds of the air come and lodge in the branches thereof.

33 Another parable spake he unto them; The kingdom of heaven is like unto leaven, which a woman took, and hid in three measures of meal, till the whole was leavened.

Matthew 20:1-16 (KJV)

1 For the kingdom of heaven is like unto a man that is an householder, which went out early in the morning to hire labourers into his vineyard.

2 And when he had agreed with the labourers for a penny a day, he sent them into his vineyard.

-59-

3 And he went out about the third hour, and saw others standing idle in the marketplace,

4 And said unto them; Go ye also into the vineyard, and whatsoever is right I will give you. And they went their way.

5 Again he went out about the sixth and ninth hour, and did likewise.

6 And about the eleventh hour he went out, and found others standing idle, and saith unto them, Why stand ye here all the day idle?

7 They say unto him, Because no man hath hired us. He saith unto them, Go ye also into the vineyard; and whatsoever is right, that shall ye receive.

8 So when even was come, the lord of the vineyard saith unto his steward, Call the labourers, and give them their hire, beginning from the last unto the first.

9 And when they came that were hired about the eleventh hour, they received every man a penny.

10 But when the first came, they supposed that they should have received more; and they likewise received every man a penny.

11 And when they had received it, they murmured against the goodman of the house,

12 Saying, These last have wrought but one hour, and thou hast made them equal unto us, which have borne the burden and heat of the day.

13 But he answered one of them, and said, Friend, I do thee no wrong: didst not thou agree with me for a penny?

14 Take that thine is, and go thy way: I will give unto this last, even as unto thee.

[15] Is it not lawful for me to do what I will with mine own? Is thine eye evil, because I am good?
[16] So the last shall be first, and the first last: for many be called, but few chosen.

Matthew 24:14 (KJV)
[14] And this gospel of the kingdom shall be preached in all the world for a witness unto all nations; and then shall the end come.

Matthew 25:1-30 (KJV)
[1] Then shall the kingdom of heaven be likened unto ten virgins, which took their lamps, and went forth to meet the bridegroom.
[2] And five of them were wise, and five were foolish.
[3] They that were foolish took their lamps, and took no oil with them:
[4] But the wise took oil in their vessels with their lamps.
[5] While the bridegroom tarried, they all slumbered and slept.
[6] And at midnight there was a cry made, Behold, the bridegroom cometh; go ye out to meet him.
[7] Then all those virgins arose, and trimmed their lamps.
[8] And the foolish said unto the wise, Give us of your oil; for our lamps are gone out.
[9] But the wise answered, saying, Not so; lest there be not enough for us and you: but go ye rather to them that sell, and buy for yourselves.
[10] And while they went to buy, the bridegroom came; and they that were ready went in with him to the marriage: and the door was shut.
[11] Afterward came also the other virgins, saying, Lord, Lord, open to us.
[12] But he answered and said, Verily I say unto you, I know you not.

-61-

13 Watch therefore, for ye know neither the day nor the hour wherein the Son of man cometh.

14 For the kingdom of heaven is as a man travelling into a far country, who called his own servants, and delivered unto them his goods.

15 And unto one he gave five talents, to another two, and to another one; to every man according to his several ability; and straightway took his journey.

16 Then he that had received the five talents went and traded with the same, and made them other five talents.

17 And likewise he that had received two, he also gained other two.

18 But he that had received one went and digged in the earth, and hid his lord's money.

19 After a long time the lord of those servants cometh, and reckoneth with them.

20 And so he that had received five talents came and brought other five talents, saying, Lord, thou deliveredst unto me five talents: behold, I have gained beside them five talents more.

21 His lord said unto him, Well done, thou good and faithful servant: thou hast been faithful over a few things, I will make thee ruler over many things: enter thou into the joy of thy lord.

22 He also that had received two talents came and said, Lord, thou deliveredst unto me two talents: behold, I have gained two other talents beside them.

23 His lord said unto him, Well done, good and faithful servant; thou hast been faithful over a few things, I will make thee ruler over many things: enter thou into the joy of thy lord.

24 Then he which had received the one talent came and said, Lord, I knew thee that thou art an hard man, reaping where thou hast not sown, and gathering where thou hast not strawed:
25 And I was afraid, and went and hid thy talent in the earth: lo, there thou hast that is thine.
26 His lord answered and said unto him, Thou wicked and slothful servant, thou knewest that I reap where I sowed not, and gather where I have not strawed:
27 Thou oughtest therefore to have put my money to the exchangers, and then at my coming I should have received mine own with usury.
28 Take therefore the talent from him, and give it unto him which hath ten talents.
29 For unto every one that hath shall be given, and he shall have abundance: but from him that hath not shall be taken away even that which he hath.
30 And cast ye the unprofitable servant into outer darkness: there shall be weeping and gnashing of teeth.

Love You - Not Your Sin

Romans 1:26-27 (KJV)

Romans 1:26-27 (KJV)

[26] For this cause God gave them up unto vile affections: for even their women did change the natural use into that which is against nature:

[27] And likewise also the men, leaving the natural use of the woman, burned in their lust one toward another; men with men working that which is unseemly, and receiving in themselves that recompence of their error which was meet.

Only Human!

II Corinthians 5:17, 6:16 (KJV)

II Corinthians 5:17 (KJV)
[17] Therefore if any man be in Christ, he is a new creature: old things are passed away; behold, all things are become new.

II Corinthians 6:16 (KJV)
[16] And what agreement hath the temple of God with idols? for ye are the temple of the living God; as God hath said, I will dwell in them, and walk in them; and I will be their God, and they shall be my people.

Pro-Choice?

Mark 3:4; Exodus 20:13 (KJV)

Mark 3:4 (KJV)
4 And he saith unto them, Is it lawful to do good on the sabbath days, or to do evil? to save life, or to kill? But they held their peace.

Exodus 20:13 (KJV)
13 Thou shalt not kill.

Puzzling

Genesis 1:26 (KJV)

Genesis 1:26 (KJV)
[26] And God said, Let us make man in our image, after our likeness: and let them have dominion over the fish of the sea, and over the fowl of the air, and over the cattle, and over all the earth, and over every creeping thing that creepeth upon the earth.

Sabbath Day

Exodus 20:8-11; Luke 6:5 (KJV)

Exodus 20:8-11 (KJV)

8 Remember the sabbath day, to keep it holy.

9 Six days shalt thou labour, and do all thy work:

10 But the seventh day is the sabbath of the LORD thy God: in it thou shalt not do any work, thou, nor thy son, nor thy daughter, thy manservant, nor thy maidservant, nor thy cattle, nor thy stranger that is within thy gates:

11 For in six days the LORD made heaven and earth, the sea, and all that in them is, and rested the seventh day: wherefore the LORD blessed the sabbath day, and hallowed it.

Luke 6:5 (KJV)

5 And he said unto them, That the Son of man is Lord also of the sabbath.

Seeds of Self-Destruction

James 1:26, 3:5-10; Proverbs 18:21, 25:23 (KJV)

James 1:26 (KJV)

26 If any man among you seem to be religious, and bridleth not his tongue, but deceiveth his own heart, this man's religion is vain.

James 3:5-10 (KJV)

5 Even so the tongue is a little member, and boasteth great things. Behold, how great a matter a little fire kindleth!

6 And the tongue is a fire, a world of iniquity: so is the tongue among our members, that it defileth the whole body, and setteth on fire the course of nature; and it is set on fire of hell.

7 For every kind of beasts, and of birds, and of serpents, and of things in the sea, is tamed, and hath been tamed of mankind:

8 But the tongue can no man tame; it is an unruly evil, full of deadly poison.

9 Therewith bless we God, even the Father; and therewith curse we men, which are made after the similitude of God.

10 Out of the same mouth proceedeth blessing and cursing. My brethren, these things ought not so to be.

Proverbs 18:21 (KJV)

21 Death and life are in the power of the tongue: and they that love it shall eat the fruit thereof.

Proverbs 25:23 (KJV)

23 The north wind driveth away rain: so doth an angry countenance a backbiting tongue.

Take No Thought

Luke 12:22-30 (KJV)

Luke 12:22-30 (KJV)

[22] And he said unto his disciples, Therefore I say unto you, Take no thought for your life, what ye shall eat; neither for the body, what ye shall put on.

[23] The life is more than meat, and the body is more than raiment.

[24] Consider the ravens: for they neither sow nor reap; which neither have storehouse nor barn; and God feedeth them: how much more are ye better than the fowls?

[25] And which of you with taking thought can add to his stature one cubit?

[26] If ye then be not able to do that thing which is least, why take ye thought for the rest?

[27] Consider the lilies how they grow: they toil not, they spin not; and yet I say unto you, that Solomon in all his glory was not arrayed like one of these.

[28] If then God so clothe the grass, which is to day in the field, and to morrow is cast into the oven; how much more will he clothe you, O ye of little faith?

[29] And seek not ye what ye shall eat, or what ye shall drink, neither be ye of doubtful mind.

[30] For all these things do the nations of the world seek after: and your Father knoweth that ye have need of these things.

There But For the Grace...

Luke 10:27-37; Matthew 22:39 (KJV)

Luke 10:27-37 (KJV)

27 And he answering said, Thou shalt love the Lord thy God with all thy heart, and with all thy soul, and with all thy strength, and with all thy mind; and thy neighbour as thyself.

28 And he said unto him, Thou hast answered right: this do, and thou shalt live.

29 But he, willing to justify himself, said unto Jesus, And who is my neighbour?

30 And Jesus answering said, A certain man went down from Jerusalem to Jericho, and fell among thieves, which stripped him of his raiment, and wounded him, and departed, leaving him half dead.

31 And by chance there came down a certain priest that way: and when he saw him, he passed by on the other side.

32 And likewise a Levite, when he was at the place, came and looked on him, and passed by on the other side.

33 But a certain Samaritan, as he journeyed, came where he was: and when he saw him, he had compassion on him,

34 And went to him, and bound up his wounds, pouring in oil and wine, and set him on his own beast, and brought him to an inn, and took care of him.

35 And on the morrow when he departed, he took out two pence, and gave them to the host, and said unto him, Take care of him; and whatsoever thou spendest more, when I come again, I will repay thee.

36 Which now of these three, thinkest thou, was neighbour unto him that fell among the thieves?

37 And he said, He that shewed mercy on him. Then said Jesus unto him, Go, and do thou likewise.

-71-

Matthew 22:39 (KJV)
[39] And the second is like unto it, Thou shalt love thy neighbour as thyself.

Tower of Babel

Genesis 11:1-10 (KJV)

Genesis 11:1-10 (KJV)

1 And the whole earth was of one language, and of one speech.

2 And it came to pass, as they journeyed from the east, that they found a plain in the land of Shinar; and they dwelt there.

3 And they said one to another, Go to, let us make brick, and burn them thoroughly. And they had brick for stone, and slime had they for morter.

4 And they said, Go to, let us build us a city and a tower, whose top may reach unto heaven; and let us make us a name, lest we be scattered abroad upon the face of the whole earth.

5 And the LORD came down to see the city and the tower, which the children of men builded.

6 And the LORD said, Behold, the people is one, and they have all one language; and this they begin to do: and now nothing will be restrained from them, which they have imagined to do.

7 Go to, let us go down, and there confound their language, that they may not understand one another's speech.

8 So the LORD scattered them abroad from thence upon the face of all the earth: and they left off to build the city.

9 Therefore is the name of it called Babel; because the LORD did there confound the language of all the earth: and from thence did the LORD scatter them abroad upon the face of all the earth.

10 These are the generations of Shem: Shem was an hundred years old, and begat Arphaxad two years after the flood:

True Way of Life

John 13:34-35, 14:6 (KJV)

John 13:34-35 (KJV)
[34] A new commandment I give unto you, That ye love one another; as I have loved you, that ye also love one another.
[35] By this shall all men know that ye are my disciples, if ye have love one to another.

John 14:6 (KJV)
[6] Jesus saith unto him, I am the way, the truth, and the life: no man cometh unto the Father, but by me.

Dr. Lydia A. Woods

What's Your Problem?

Mark 16:15-18 (KJV)

Mark 16:15-18 (KJV)
15 And he said unto them, Go ye into all the world, and preach the gospel to every creature.
16 He that believeth and is baptized shall be saved; but he that believeth not shall be damned.
17 And these signs shall follow them that believe; In my name shall they cast out devils; they shall speak with new tongues;
18 They shall take up serpents; and if they drink any deadly thing, it shall not hurt them; they shall lay hands on the sick, and they shall recover.

-75-

Scriptural Index

I Peter
2:9
  Call My Name, 5, 49
5:3
  If You Will Be Great, 17, 59

Revelations
22:13
  Ain't He All That!, 1, 47

www.ingramcontent.com/pod-product-compliance
Lightning Source LLC
Chambersburg PA
CBHW071832020426
42331CB00007B/1691